SUPER-AWESOME SCIENCE

THE SCIENCE OF
MUSIC

by Cecilia Pinto McCarthy

Content Consultant
Elizabeth Margulis, PhD
Professor
University of Arkansas

Core Library

An Imprint of Abdo Publishing
abdopublishing.com

abdopublishing.com

Published by Abdo Publishing, a division of ABDO, PO Box 398166, Minneapolis, Minnesota 55439. Copyright © 2017 by Abdo Consulting Group, Inc. International copyrights reserved in all countries. No part of this book may be reproduced in any form without written permission from the publisher. Core Library™ is a trademark and logo of Abdo Publishing.

Printed in the United States of America, North Mankato, Minnesota
032016
092016

THIS BOOK CONTAINS
RECYCLED MATERIALS

Cover Photo: Matt Crossick/PA Wire URN:19751849/AP Images
Interior Photos: Matt Crossick/PA Wire URN:19751849/AP Images, 1; Charles Sykes/Invision/ AP Images, 4; Hurst Photo/Shutterstock Images, 6; Shutterstock Images, 9, 15, 27 (bottom), 39; Christian Bertrand/Shutterstock Images, 10; Chris Pizzello/AP Images, 12; Mohamad Torokman/ Reuters, 17; Marcus Andreassen/Gonzalez Photo/The Hell Gate/Corbis, 18; Dafydd Owen/ Retna/Photoshot/Newscom, 21; Cristi Kerekes/Shutterstock Images, 22; Rex Features/AP Images, 24, 43; Alila Medical Media/Shutterstock Images, 27 (top); Zeduce/Corbis, 29; KGC-243/STAR MAX/IPx/AP Images, 30, 45; Martin Novak/Shutterstock Images, 32; Jill Toyoshiba/ The Kansas City Star/AP Images, 35; Amanda Cowan/The Columbian/AP Images, 37

Editor: Jon Westmark
Series Designer: Jake Nordby

Cataloging-in-Publication Data
Names: McCarthy, Cecilia Pinto, author.
Title: The science of music / by Cecilia Pinto McCarthy.
Description: Minneapolis, MN : Abdo Publishing, [2017] | Series: Super-awesome science | Includes bibliographical references and index.
Identifiers: LCCN 2015960502 | ISBN 9781680782486 (lib. bdg.) | ISBN 9781680776591 (ebook)
Subjects: LCSH: Music--Juvenile literature.
Classification: DDC 534--dc23
LC record available at http://lccn.loc.gov/2015960502

CONTENTS

MUSIC IS VIBRATION

It's a Saturday night, and thousands of screaming fans are crowded into a stadium. On stage a singer holds a microphone and fills the air with her energetic melody. Beside her the twangs of an electric guitar boom from giant, vibrating speakers. The sound waves resonate all the way to the seats in the back row. Listeners clap in time with the beat. Hours later they will still hear the sounds of the music in their ears.

Music performers use technology so they can be heard by thousands of fans in concert.

Sound travels through vibrations. The human ear and brain hear these vibrations as sound.

What Is Sound?

Sound is a type of energy made from a vibrating source. When something vibrates, its particles move back and forth. The particles do not move far. Instead they bump into others nearby. In turn those particles bump into those around them. The energy gets transferred outward.

This movement of energy is called a sound wave. Unlike waves on a lake or ocean, sound waves do not drift up and down. Instead, sound waves move back and forth like an accordion. Sound waves create areas where there are many particles close together and areas where there are few particles together.

Not all sound waves are the same. Some waves carry a lot of energy and push many particles together. But just because a wave carries a lot of energy does not mean it will sound loud. The person hearing the sound determines its loudness. A sound may seem loud to one person and not to another. A sound's intensity is measured in

Silent Space

Sound travels when air molecules bump into one another. A vacuum is an area without air molecules. Outer space is a vacuum. No sound can travel there. Two astronauts floating next to each other in space would not be able to hear each other, even if they could speak through their thick suits. Astronauts can hear one another inside spacecraft. That's because there is air inside the craft.

units called decibels (dB). Sounds that are too intense can cause hearing loss in people.

Sound waves also have different frequencies. Frequency is how quickly particles move back and forth. Something that vibrates at a high frequency creates a high-pitched sound. When something vibrates more slowly, it creates a low-pitched sound. Frequency is measured in units called hertz (Hz). A hertz equals one vibration per second. The human ear can hear sounds between 20 and 20,000 Hz.

IN THE REAL WORLD

Hearing Loss

In 2015 the World Health Organization (WHO) issued a warning. It stated that 1.1 billion people from 12 to 35 years old were damaging their hearing. The WHO found that many young people listen to music at unsafe levels for long periods of time. Listening to music at 100 dB for longer than 15 minutes can cause hearing damage. The WHO recommends keeping the volume of personal audio devices below 60 percent of the maximum volume. Smartphone apps can also help monitor safe listening levels.

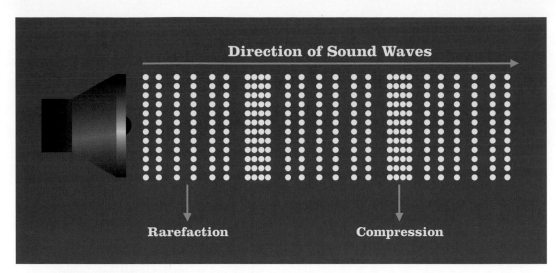

Direction of Sound Waves

Rarefaction

Compression

Wave Patterns

This diagram shows sound waves moving through the air. The yellow dots represent air particles. When the particles in the wave are close together, it is called a compression. When they are far apart, it is called a rarefaction. What would the wave pattern look like if the frequency were higher? What if the intensity were higher?

Sound waves can be arranged into patterns. We control patterns of sound to communicate through speech. We also create music in this way. Music is the art of controlling patterns of sound.

Art Meets Science

In the 500s BCE, a Greek mathematician named Pythagoras studied music. He wanted to know about the connections between music, math, and science.

Harps contain dozens of strings of different length.

Pythagoras played a stringed instrument. He noticed that when he plucked strings of the same length, tightness, and thickness, they made the same pitch. The strings sounded consonant, or pleasing, together. When Pythagoras changed the length of one of the strings and not the other, the pitches did not sound consonant. They sounded dissonant, or bad, together. But Pythagoras found that certain intervals, or combinations of pitches, sounded nice. He found he could mathematically determine which pitches would sound good together. Pythagoras developed the first mathematically based scale, or series of pitches. He created instruments with strings that played consonant intervals.

People have continued to learn about the connections between science and music. A singer may not think about the science of music during a performance. But scientific principles help us find new ways to make and interact with music.

FURTHER EVIDENCE

Chapter One discusses sound waves. What are some of the main ideas of this chapter? The website at the link below also discusses sound and music. How does the information on the website support the ideas in Chapter One? What new information does it present?

Becoming Part of the Music
mycorelibrary.com/science-of-music

CHAPTER TWO

MAKING MUSIC WITH INSTRUMENTS

Humans have been making musical instruments for thousands of years. Some of the earliest instruments were flutes. They are thought to be at least 35,000 years old. These early flutes were made of bones from vultures and ivory from mammoth tusks.

Today people use many types of instruments to make music. These include string, wind, brass,

Instruments have changed greatly as technology has advanced.

percussion, and even electronic instruments. In order to create music, most instruments must have three basic elements: a source, a resonator, and a radiator. The sound source is the part of the instrument that vibrates to make sound waves. The sound resonator amplifies notes, or makes them louder. Then the instrument's radiator spreads the sound waves out so they travel through the air.

Strings

Stringed instruments make sound when their strings are bowed, strummed, plucked, or struck. Violins, violas, cellos, double basses, and guitars are stringed instruments. The strings are different thicknesses. Thick, heavy strings vibrate slowly and make low-pitched notes. Thin, light strings vibrate quickly. They make higher notes. Stringed instruments have pegs that players turn to tighten and loosen strings. Changing the how tight the strings are changes how quickly they vibrate.

String players can put a rubber piece called a mute on the bridge to lessen the vibration. Playing with a mute results in a softer sound.

When players bow or pluck a string, they apply a force to the string. The force vibrates the string, which is the sound source. But by itself a plucked string does not make much sound. The rest of the instrument helps make the sound louder. The strings rest on a special carved piece called the bridge. The string's vibrations travel to the bridge. They then go to the wooden body of the instrument. Inside, a sound

IN THE REAL WORLD

Vegetable Orchestra

Vienna, Austria, is home to a unique orchestra. The Vegetable Orchestra is made up of artists who use kitchen knives, drills, and other tools to carve vegetables into musical instruments. They make carrot flutes, pumpkin drums, pepper horns, and eggplant clappers. Vegetable instruments lose their freshness over time. The musicians must remake almost all their instruments before each concert. Microphones and amplifiers help the instruments project their sounds. After concerts the orchestra's cook serves the audience soup made from the leftover vegetables. The orchestra has performed around the world.

post carries vibrations to the instrument's back. The top and bottom of the instrument act as resonators. So does the air inside the body. Finally sound radiates through holes on the instrument's top. String players press on the strings with their fingers. This changes the string length and makes different pitches.

Winds

Woodwind, or wind, instruments make sound when a player blows air into the instrument. The mouthpieces of some wind instruments

Flutists blow air across a hole to create sound.

contain reeds. Reeds are the sound source. Blowing into the mouthpiece makes the reed vibrate. Other woodwinds, such as flutes, do not have reeds. The player blows air across a hole. The air splits along the edge of the hole. The vibrations travel through the column of air inside the instrument. The body of the instrument acts as the resonator.

To play notes, woodwind players cover holes along the instrument with their fingers or press down metal keys. Opening and closing the holes changes

Tubas have long sections of tubing, resulting in a lower sound than other winds.

how far the air travels. The changes in the length of the air column make different notes.

Brass

Many brass instruments, such as trumpet and trombone, have systems of tubes. The tubes create different routes the air can travel through. Trumpet players use keys to control how the air goes through the instrument. Trombones have tubing that the player slides in and out. Moving the slide changes the length of the column of air. As a player moves the slide, the trombone plays different notes. The bell at the end of brass instruments radiates the sound.

Percussion

There are many instruments in the percussion family. Drums and cymbals are types of percussion instruments. They make sound when they are struck, shaken, or rubbed. The human body can also be a percussion instrument. Clapping hands, stomping feet, and snapping fingers are all sources of sound.

Some percussion instruments are tuned to certain notes. One example is the stretched material on top of the timpani drum. It can be loosened or tightened to play an exact pitch. Striking the timpani creates vibrations across the head. The vibrations travel to the body of the drum. The body resonates along with the air inside the drum. Sound then radiates through the material stretched across the head of the drum.

Resonance

All objects have a natural frequency at which they vibrate. The stretched material on the head of a drum is elastic. When the frequency of the vibrations caused by the drummer's strike match the natural frequency of the drumhead, there is a huge increase in the height of the sound wave. This increase is known as resonance. Resonance allows sound waves to project out more from the instrument.

Electronic Music

Technology has changed the world of music. Electronic instruments called synthesizers use electricity to copy the sounds of other instruments. They can also make new sounds. Many of today's musical artists use electronics to make music or change the way their music sounds.

In the early 1930s, inventor George Beauchamp and engineer Adolph Rickenbacker began making electric guitars. Unlike acoustic guitars, many electric guitars have solid bodies. This means the body does not add much to the instrument's sound. Instead the electric guitar uses an amplifier to

Synthesizers allow musicians to use one device to make many different sounds.

make its sound louder. Strings on the electric guitar rest on rows of pickups. The pickups are magnets wrapped by thousands of coils of a thin copper wire. Electricity travels easily through copper. The magnets create a magnetic field. When the guitar's metal strings are strummed, they vibrate. The vibrations cause the magnetic field to move. This makes an electric current. The current goes through a cable to an amplifier. The amplifier boosts the electric signal and sends it to a speaker.

Speakers emit sound by disturbing the air particles nearby.

The speaker uses electromagnets to turn electric current back into vibrations. The vibrations move a speaker cone in and out. This creates changes in air pressure. The changes are sound waves.

Speakers come in different sizes. Small ones, called tweeters, are designed for high-frequency sound waves that move quickly back and forth. Large ones, called woofers, are for the slower motion of low-frequency sounds.

Synthesizers are electronic instruments. Inventor Robert Moog made many early synthesizers. An article in the *New York Times* described how the instruments work:

> *The first Moog synthesizers were collections of modules . . . . The first module, an oscillator, would produce a sound wave, giving a musician a choice of several kinds. . . . The wave was sent to the next module . . . with which the player defined the way a note begins and ends, and how long it is held. A note might, for example, explode in a sudden burst, like a trumpet blast, or it could fade in at any number of speeds. From there, the sound went to a third module, a filter, which was used to shape its color and texture. Using these modules, and others that Mr. Moog went on to create, a musician could either imitate acoustic instruments, or create purely electronic sounds.*

> Source: Allan Kozinn. "Robert Moog, Creator of Music Synthesizer, Dies at 71." International New York Times. *The New York Times Company, August 23, 2005. Accessed January 27, 2016.*

What's the Big Idea?

Take a close look at this passage. How is the process of making sound with electronic instruments different from other instruments? What does the synthesizer allow musicians to do that other instruments do not?

MAKING MUSIC WITH VOICE

usic is not music until it is heard by the human ear and understood by the human brain. Before that it is simply sound. As sound waves travel, some are caught by the outer part of the ear, called the pinna. The waves continue down the ear canal and strike the eardrum. The eardrum vibrates. It passes the vibrations on to three tiny bones. Next the vibrations reach the cochlea, a curled

The human brain receives and evaluates sounds almost instantly.

Aids and Implants

People with hearing loss can benefit from hearing aids and cochlear implants. These devices change sound waves into electric signals. Hearing aids are worn on or inside the ear. They work by picking up sound and making it louder. People who are deaf or very hard of hearing use cochlear implants. These are different from hearing aids. They do not make sound louder. The implant has two parts. One part is placed behind the ear. It picks up sounds. The sounds are sent as signals to the part located inside the ear. The signals eventually reach the brain. The brain interprets the signals as sound.

tube in the inner ear. The liquid-filled cochlea has hairs that respond to sound. They pick up the vibrations and send signals to the brain. The brain reads the signals as sound.

The Human Voice

The human body not only hears music but also makes music. The larynx is an organ in the front of the neck on top of the windpipe. Inside the larynx are two vocal folds. These folds are the sound source for the human voice.

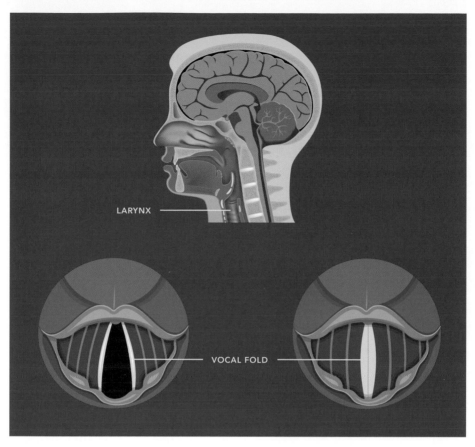

LARYNX

VOCAL FOLD

Vocal Folds

The vocal folds are located in the larynx. Which diagram shows the vocal folds of a speaking or singing person?

When a person breathes out, air travels from the lungs into the larynx. When there is no speech, the vocal folds are relaxed and open. But during talking and singing, the larynx muscles tighten. This brings the vocal folds together. As the air passes between the closed vocal folds, they vibrate and make sound.

Vocal fold vibrations can range from approximately 100 to 1,000 times per second. The pitch of the sound depends on the length and tension of the vocal folds. People with low voices have longer vocal folds that tend to vibrate more slowly. The faster the vocal folds vibrate, the higher the pitch becomes. Men's vocal-fold vibrations average approximately 125 Hz when talking. Women's vocal folds vibrate at an average of 200 Hz. Most children's voices are approximately 300 Hz.

IN THE REAL WORLD

Damaged Voices

Hours of singing on tour can take a toll on a singer's throat and vocal folds. Vocal folds may grow lesions that change how they vibrate. This can make a singer hoarse. Singers such as Keith Urban, Adele, and Sam Smith have had surgery to fix throat or vocal-fold damage. New medical techniques help to treat vocal fold problems before they become permanent. Imaging machines allow doctors to see growths or bleeding sooner. Better lasers can stop bleeding without causing scars that could ruin a singer's voice.

Soprano is the voice type that can reach the highest frequency. Sopranos can sing upward of 1,500 Hz.

Some performers wear wireless microphones in order to move around stage. Wireless microphones turn sound into radio signals.

The larynx and vocal folds get help from other body parts to make sound. The chest, throat, nose, and mouth act as resonators. They make sounds louder.

People can also use microphones. A microphone picks up sound waves made by a voice. The vibrations transfer to a thin piece of plastic inside the microphone. Behind the plastic is a coil wrapped around a magnet. The vibrations make the coil move back and forth, creating an electric current. The current flows from the microphone through wires to an amplifier. Finally the amplifier boosts the signal and transfers it to a loudspeaker.

EXPLORE ONLINE

Chapter Three discusses how the human ear hears sound. The website below also describes how the ear works. Look through the website below. How does human hearing differ from that of animals? What new information about ears and hearing did you learn from the website?

Biology of Hearing
mycorelibrary.com/science-of-music

CHAPTER FOUR

MUSIC AND THE MIND

The human brain is made up of three main parts: the cerebrum, the cerebellum, and the brain stem. Within each of these main parts are areas that control body functions and emotions. Tasks such as speaking, moving, and breathing are controlled by different parts of the brain. But musical activities use the whole brain. There is no single music area.

Reading music and playing an instrument activate different parts of the brain.

Listening, playing, and composing music each use many parts of the brain.

The human brain is capable of changing. It continues to make neurons into adulthood. Neurons are cells that send signals through the brain. Human brains have billions of neurons. They communicate with one another. As people learn, brain cells change. They create more receptors that can receive signals.

Music benefits the brain by stimulating it to create new connections. Playing a musical instrument has the greatest effect on the brain. To play an instrument, a person often must read music, move body parts, and listen to notes. These activities use several parts of the brain at once. When a musician practices an instrument, more connections form between the two halves of the brain. This allows the brain to communicate more quickly. Musical training improves hearing and speech skills, memory, attention, reading, and physical control.

Playing music at a young age can help language development.

Music, Emotion, and Health

Music activates the brain and causes the human body to respond in different ways. When a person hears music, it creates a number of bodily reactions. First the nervous system is activated. Information from the ears is sent to the brain stem and other sound-processing areas.

The brain stem's job is to process information that has to do with sound, emotions, heart rate, breathing, movement, and other functions. The brain stem responds to sound automatically. It evaluates the frequencies of the sound. If frequencies sound good, neurons near the brain stem release chemicals such as dopamine. These chemicals help create feelings of pleasure.

For All Ages

Babies respond to music even before birth. When loud music is played to unborn babies, their heart rates increase. They move their bodies more. Soft music causes them to keep still. It helps control babies' heartbeats. When quiet music is played to premature babies, they calm down. They also sleep and eat

Some hospitals use music therapy to help stabilize infants' heartbeats and breathing. Music therapy is also used for pain management in newborns.

better. Doctors use this knowledge to treat sick and premature infants.

Music also affects how adults feel. People can sense the emotional expression of music. Slow, quiet, low-pitched music is understood as sad. Quick, high-pitched music seems happy. The human body mimics the emotion of the music. This happens because the human brain responds to music in much the same way it responds to hearing a human voice. When someone is angry, the person's voice may be loud, fast, and intense. Music that is also loud, fast, and intense creates the same response in the brain.

This emotional connection to music can help people who are ill. It causes the brain to release chemicals that create good feelings. Soft music relaxes breathing and heart rate and reduces stress. Many hospitals play music to help lower patients' pain and stress.

Music and Daily Life

Listening to music also affects areas across the brain that control movement and memory. Music is closely connected with experiences. Singing or listening to music stimulates parts of the brain to recall past memories. Advertisers use this connection between music and memory to sell products. Short songs and jingles are easy to remember. People learn to link products with songs they hear in ads. Different music

Some people use energetic music to help motivate them to exercise.

can be used in advertising to capture the attention of people of a particular age or group. For example, a company selling sports cars might play music that appeals to young people.

Storeowners also use music to influence how customers spend their time and money. Customers

Earworms

Earworm is the term used to describe when a catchy tune repeats over and over in a person's mind. Some scientists believe that earworms are a type of automatic musical memory. But no one knows for sure how or why people get earworms. Earworms tend to happen more often when a person is doing something that requires little thinking, such as walking. One way to end an earworm is by distracting the brain with a difficult activity, such as solving a puzzle. Another solution is to chew gum. Chewing works because it is a movement that disturbs the brain's automatic memory process.

relax when background music with a slow tempo is played. A relaxed customer is likely to spend more time and therefore more money in a store.

Music and humans have been bound together for thousands of years. Every human culture has music. Music has the ability to change our brains, shape our emotions, control how we act, and improve our lives. It is a vital piece of everyday life.

Music has the power to influence emotions and change lives. Author Stacy Horn wrote about singing's effects in *TIME*:

> *When you sing, musical vibrations move through you, altering your physical and emotional landscape. Group singing . . . is the most exhilarating and transformative of all. It takes something incredibly intimate, a sound that begins inside you, shares it with a roomful of people and it comes back as something even more thrilling: harmony. So it's not surprising that group singing is on the rise. According to Chorus America, 32.5 million adults sing in choirs, up by almost 10 million over the past six years. . . . The elation may come from endorphins, a hormone released by singing, which is associated with feelings of pleasure. Or it might be from oxytocin, another hormone released during singing, which has been found to alleviate anxiety and stress.*

Source: Stacy Horn. "Singing Changes Your Brain." TIME. Time Inc., August 16, 2013. Accessed January 27, 2016.

Back It Up

This passage discusses the benefits of singing as part of a group. The author of this passage uses specific evidence to support her point. Write a paragraph describing the author's point. Then write down two or three pieces of evidence the author uses to support her point.

- Sound comes from a vibrating object and travels in waves through the air.
- Music is sound made by organized, repeated patterns of vibrations.
- Different speeds of vibration produce different pitches.
- Frequency is the rate of vibration.
- Intensity describes the amount of energy in sound waves.
- Instruments use vibrations from strings, air, wood, metal, and other materials to create sound.
- Music is not music until it is processed by the human brain.

- People use vocal cords and other parts of their bodies to make sounds and music.
- Music has the power to alter the human brain and change how humans act and feel.

STOP AND THINK

Tell the Tale

Chapter Three of this book discusses how sound waves travel through the human ear and become signals that are sent to the brain. Imagine you are a musical note entering a listener's ear. Write a paragraph about your journey through the different parts of the ear and into the brain. What parts must you pass on your way?

Take a Stand

Learning to play a musical instrument has been shown to be beneficial to a child's overall learning experience. But many schools have reduced or cut their music programs. Do you think all schools should have music programs? Should all children have to learn to play a musical instrument? Why or why not?

Why Do I Care?

You may or may not sing, listen to music, or play an instrument. But you probably still hear music almost every day, maybe on the radio or on television. How does music affect your life and the lives of people you know? How would life be different without music?

You Are There

This book discusses how music affects how people feel. Think about a time that music made you feel happy, sad, or scared. Maybe you were at a party or watching a scary movie. Write a paragraph describing the situation, the music you were listening to, and how it made you feel.

GLOSSARY

amplify
to make louder

cochlea
the part of the inner ear that contains nerve endings that send sound information to the brain

frequency
the number of times a sound wave is repeated in a period of time

implant
something placed into a person's body through surgery

intensity
the amount of strength or force something has

larynx
the part of the throat that contains the vocal folds

lesion
an abnormal spot or area caused by injury or sickness

pitch
the highness or lowness of a sound

radiate
to send out

resonate
to make a loud, clear sound for a long time

vibrate
to move back and forth or from side to side

LEARN MORE

Books

Kenney, Karen Latchana. *The Science of Music: Discovering Sound*. Minneapolis, MN: Abdo, 2016.

Lock, Deborah, ed. *Children's Book of Music*. New York: DK Children, 2010.

Sjonger, Rebecca. *Maker Projects for Kids Who Love Music*. New York: Crabtree, 2016.

Websites

To learn more about Super-Awesome Science, visit **booklinks.abdopublishing.com**. These links are routinely monitored and updated to provide the most current information available.

Visit **mycorelibrary.com** for free additional tools for teachers and students.

INDEX

ABOUT THE AUTHOR

Cecilia Pinto McCarthy has written several books about science and nature. She also teaches environmental science programs at a nature sanctuary and enjoys playing the violin. She lives with her family north of Boston, Massachusetts.

21·99